The Social Media Guide for Ancestral Research

Applying Web2.0 Strategies

Claire V. Brisson-Banks, B.S., MLIS, A.G

THE SOCIAL MEDIA GUIDE TO ANCESTRAL RESEARCH
Applying Web 2.0 Strategies

© 2011 by Claire V. Brisson-Banks
ISBN 978-1-4583-8021-0

Cover Photo: ©iStockphoto.com/Nikolay Kropachev

Contact:
http://www/timelessgen.com
claire@timelessgen.com

Dedication

I dedicate this book to all ancestral seekers, my colleagues and friends, but most of all to my husband, Les, our six children; Angela, Dawn, Jessica-Anne, John, Phillip and Theresa, their spouses and our grandchildren here now and those yet to arrive on the planet. Lastly, to those on the other side whose spiritual guidance was always there, 'Thank You'.

Acknowledgement

I wish to thank my family, friends and colleagues who encouraged me to write this guide in hopes of aiding those seeking out their ancestors while struggling with new technology.

While the research steps have remained the same, the methods have improved immensely thanks to all the many individuals who are creating new programs that benefit genealogical researchers throughout the world. The variety of open source programs allow many to gather, research and store their data in the 'cloud' which is virtual space.

Additionally, many new programs allow for connecting up with previously unknown relations that often can help fill in many of the empty places in one's family tree. Their creators are to be commended for developing these programs.

Lastly, I wish to thank all who are learning and experimenting with these new applications, may they find success and continue on in the spirit of being lifelong learners, researchers and willing to take a chance in the Web 2.0 world

Table of Contents

Introduction

Investigating ones family history continues to grow in interest daily. While family history research has long been a top hobby among hobbyist, it is even more so today. The actual occupation of a genealogist can be traced back many centuries along with heraldists, lineage specialists, and family historians. Searching for ones ancestors was extremely time consuming and labor intensive during these early times.

Long before online databases, individuals searched through records manually by going to where the records were located or if they had been put on microfilm, they would look at them by ordering the film and viewing them on a microfilm reader. Despite these drawbacks, the art of searching for ones' ancestors continued to grow over the years. It really exploded in 1977 with the mini television series *Roots* which was based on Alex Haley's work *Roots: The Saga of an American Family.*

This series showed that everyone can do family history

and brought many new creative minds into the field of genealogical research which also opened the doors to the invention of new ways to accomplish this type of research. Other television shows like *Ancestors* by PBS in 1997, and more recently; *Who Do You Think You Are?*, (WDYTYA). This show aired in 2004 on BBC and was the highest-rated program of that year.

According to Dan French's article in Digital Spy, WDYTYA attracts over 6 million viewers in England and is in its eight season.[1] Its popularity has spilled over to other countries with WDYTYA in Canada in 2007, Ireland and Australia in 2008, South Africa in 2009 and the United States in 2010.

While there are other radio and television shows that have worked at capturing the essence of family history, a new player is on the scene called "Social Media". Just

---

[1] French, Dan. "Television - News - 6.4 million uncover Davina's family history - Digital Spy." Breaking celebrity, TV and showbiz news - Digital Spy. http://www.digitalspy.com/tv/news/a165437/64-million-uncover-davinas-family-history.html (accessed December 14, 2010).

the phrase itself can be confusing, however, time has shown that genealogist aid one another through their own social networking. The ability to enhance such networking with the aid of Web 2.0 technologies is the basis for this book. It is hoped that throughout the following chapters you will be able to discover and employ some of the new tools available in the genealogist's arsenal to extend and fill in your own family trees or even break through a brick wall.

Chapter 1

Social Media

Everywhere you look today the buzz words are "Social Media" or "Social Networking". While they are similar they are not the same. To assist with clarification between the two let's look at the definitions provided by *Answers.com*:

Social Media

Social media is a broad term used to describe the various tools, networks and technologies for sharing content, ideas and knowledge and connecting and collaborating online. It encompasses wikis, podcasts, blogs, social networks, forums, message boards and other viral-type platforms where communities of people come together.[2]

Social Networking

"An association of people drawn together by family, work or hobby"; the term was first coined by Professor J. A. Barnes in the 1950s,

---

[2] "Answers.com - What is social media." WikiAnswers - The Q&A wiki. http://wiki.answers.com/Q/What_is_social_media (accessed January 3, 2011).

who defined the size of a social network as a group of about 100 to 150 people.

On the Web, social networking sites such as *MySpace*, *Facebook* and *Twitter* have expanded the concept to include a company's customers, a celebrity's fans and politicians' constituents.[3]

Social Media provides the tools to take social networking to levels beyond its original concepts in order to reach out to anyone, anywhere in the world at anytime. Land boundaries and time zones along with the expense of physical travel disappear bringing into focus a whole new reality for the participants. The power behind these applications is truly amazing and the main reason they are such great assets to genealogists and family historians throughout the new world-wide community.

---

[3] "Social network: Definition from Answers.com." Answers.com: Wiki Q&A combined with free online dictionary, thesaurus, and encyclopedias. http://www.answers.com/topic/social-network (accessed January 3, 2011).

To add to this mix is the plethora of genealogical and family history information that is now available in a mixture of online database formats with some information free and some websites requiring a subscription to view their data. Add the massive amounts of user generated information from all the social media sites and you have a large collection of data in a variety of locations available online along with online resources only in the actual physical repositories.

These circumstances have created the need to devise new search methods to locate just the right data for the user's needs at the time of their search. Diane Gayeski reminds those who have followed technological advances over a number of decades that, each new communication technology introduced seems to be a stepping stone to what comes next while making learning and training easier throughout the whole process.[4] Connecting genealogical researchers together through these new applications brings about greater collaborative efforts to enhance and fill in the gaps that exist in most family trees.

Learning how to combine the typical research strategies of books, microfilm and microfiche with these new social media applications creates the perfect mix for any new and/or seasoned genealogists. The ability to access information with a few clicks of either a mouse or a hand held device brings all these applications into reality for those who are willing to venture into the digital world with an open mind and

_____

[4] Gayeski, Diane M.. "Predicting the Success of New Media for Organizational Learning." OmniCom Associates. www.dgayeski.com/predict.html (accessed January 3, 2011).

the patience to learn new ways and methods of

achieving research success.

Chapter 2

Electronic Mail and Mailing Lists

In May, 2010, American Online (AOL) celebrated 25 years of providing email services to millions of individuals since 1985. As one reflects on their first email account it is amazing to consider that individuals have been sending emails for that length of time to a large variety of family, friends and business associates. This author still maintains a *Yahoo* account set up in 1999 and recalls email addresses from a variety of services that have long gone out of business.

The advent of email could technically be the beginning of online socializing and despite the use of many other forms of communication, email remains the main stay of most businesses and individuals around the world today. Just as receiving a hand written letter from a relative with perhaps a photo of an ancestor, receiving these same items via email will bring about the same reactions of joy.

The ability to attach photos, documents, audio and video files to email has made it a very viable way of communicating without the cost of postage and the chance of it being lost in the mail. Genealogists have been using email to share data with friends and family members by emailing historical documents, photos and their genealogical files.

Using email as a point of contact does have some drawbacks; spam, attacks by viruses and email accounts being hijacked. *It is recommended when doing genealogical research online that you set up a specific online web account just for your genealogical work.* If the email received is of upmost importance you can forwarded it onto your personal email account which in essence provides you with a back up of important data.

There are many free email sites available today, some of them are: Hotmail, Yahoo, Mail.com, Gmail and many others. *About.com* has a great article about free email accounts to aid you in your selection at http://tinyurl.com/2c6psl.[5] Once you have selected and set up your email account you can subscribe to genealogically related mailing lists along with electronic message boards which allow for exchanges of genealogical information and add the expertise of all those who are also participating either on the mailing lists or the message boards.

---

[5] About Email - Find Free Email, Email Program Support, Spam Help and Tips.
http://email.about.com/od/freeemailreviews/Find_the_Best_Fre e_Email_Accounts.htm (accessed January 3, 2011).

According to their website, *RootsWeb*

maintains over 30,000 genealogical mailing lists.[6]

A browse through their mailing lists brings up

categories of:

- Surnames
- USA
- International
- Other (covers everything from Adoptions to Nobility and more)

RootsWeb also has message boards; in fact they state they have more than 161,000 boards to choose from.[7] These message boards are broken down by locality and by topics. The top five are:
- Adoptions
- Ancestry Daily News
- Cemeteries & Tombstones
- Census

---

[6] "RootsWeb.com - Genealogy mailing lists." RootsWeb.com - Genealogy mailing lists. http://lists.rootsweb.ancestry.com/ (accessed January 4, 2011).

[7] "Message Boards - rootsweb.com." Message Boards - rootsweb.com. http://boards.rootsweb.com/?o_iid=33216&o_lid=33216 (accessed January 4, 2011).

- Crime (old west, outlaws, prisoners, police, etc.)

Other great sites that provide either mailing lists or message boards are *Genealogy.com*, *Ancestry.com*, *GenForum* and others which can be located by going to *Cyndislist.com* and typing in "mailing lists" and "message boards" in her search box, it will bring up a current list of both great resources.[8]

1996-2010: Your genealogy starting point online for more than a decade!

http://www.cyndislist.com/

Either of these resources will provide you the opportunity to research your family surnames in specific places as well as topics such as cemeteries,

---

[8] Howell, Cyndi. "Cyndi's List of Genealogy Sites on the Internet." Cyndi's List of Genealogy Sites on the Internet. http://cyndislist.com/ (accessed January 4, 2011).

military, immigrations and so much more. It is worth noting that there is a time delay in the response to either of these services, however, you will receive notice when someone posts a response to your query. This author recently had an answer to a post from ten years ago and it was just the information needed to break through a brick wall.

Both these resources archive all their posts. Whether new to genealogy or someone who has been researching for awhile, the ability to search the archives is of great value. Someone may have already asked a question it was answered by another person with just the piece of information needed to solve a mystery in the family tree being researched.

Chapter 3

Instant Messaging, SMS, Twitter

Instant Messaging

The need to communicate is inherent in all and starts from birth with face to face interactions. Communication skills are first taught at home and continue on through education, work and living. Communication methods expanded beyond the written word through letters when the telephone was invented to assist bringing people together who were physically miles apart. While telephones are still a very important of everyday life, they are now portable making it possible to talk too just about anyone, anywhere, at anytime. *Ask.com* provides the following definition of IM:

> IM falls under the umbrella term *online chat*, as it is a real-time text based networked communication system, but is distinct in that it is bases on clients that facilitate connections

between known users (often using "Buddy List", "Friend List" or "Contact List"), whereas online 'chat' also includes web-based applications that allow communication between (often anonymous) users in a multi-user environment.[9]

Instant messaging is heavily used by a large variety of businesses as well as individuals in everyday life. For businesses it is a way of providing quicker and improved services, for individuals it is a way to 'chat online' while working on other projects. Early versions of IM only allowed for the exchange of words, however, currently an individual can send a photo, a video clip, a document or just about anything through IM which opens up its usage even more.

The ability to have group chats can be quite helpful when needing assistance or advice from others.

_____

[9] "Instant messaging | Ask.com Encyclopedia." Ask.com - What's Your Question?. http://www.ask.com/wiki/Instant_messaging (accessed January 6, 2011).

Whether it is deciphering old English script in an 18th century will, needing help with reading a faded tombstone or joining in an open discussion on the problems with census records, chats through instant messaging services on PCs can be very valuable.

It is worth noting that these chats can be saved and referred to for future reference if needed. Some of the more well-known IM services are *MSN Messenger*, *AOL Instant Messenger* (AIM), *Google Talk*, *Trillian* and *Meebo*. Each of these services are free to use and can easily become another great genealogical resource.

Short Message Service (SMS) aka Text Messaging

SMS allows an individual to leave the PC behind, pick up a cell phone and send a text message to another cell phone recipient.

SearchMobileComputing.com explains text messaging this way:

SMS (Short Message Service), commonly referred to as "text messaging," is a service for sending short messages of up to 160 characters (224 characters if using a 5-bit mode) to mobile devices, including cellular phones, smartphones and PDAs.[10]

Because of the wide variety of handheld devices, there is a large variety of text messaging services available today. While most personal computer IM services are free, text messaging services are fee based and can usually be included in a cell phone package plan.

One of the problems with text messaging has been the varying types of keyboards. This has caused a new set of abbreviations when texting between individuals. This has created the emergence of

_____

[10] "What is Short Message Service (SMS)? - Definition from Whatis.com." Mobile Computing information, news and tips - SearchMobileComputing.com. http://searchmobilecomputing.techtarget.com/definition/Short-Message-Service (accessed January 6, 2011).

dictionaries for texting and/or IM; however, there are also online references to these abbreviations. *Webopedia* provides a lengthy list for those who are curious or just may want to know what some specific cryptic letters meant that were seen in a text or an IM, the URL is

http://www.webopedia.com/quick_ref/textmessageab breviations.asp.

Text messaging has become a very convenient not only for the youth today but for individuals of all ages. The ability to add a photo or a video has made texting even more valuable. Recently the author was in a cemetery and looking for a specific grave of an ancestor. Thinking the correct one was found but not quite able to read the stone, a picture of it was taken and sent onto a colleague who was able to quickly confirm it was the correct tombstone, provide all the details on the tombstone and added the GPS location

so that it could be uploaded to *FindAGrave.com*. This

was done in a matter of minutes.

The possibilities are endless when considering a

visit to a repository, the archives or an out of the way

small library where they have the only full collection of

that area's city directories that have not been scanned

or digitized.

Twitter

Twitter is also considered in the family of SMS

but is also known as micro-blogging. The original

definition of SMS mentioned "short messages of up to

160 characters"; *tweets* can only be 140 characters in

length. This could be reminiscent of telegrams, short

and to the point.

Another difference with these short messages and text messages or even IMs is that these tweets are going out to all who are following that person or that topic of messages. While it is possible to send a private tweet, it is not the general intent. It is more of a way to share information, knowledge and what is going on that could be of interest to a large number of individuals. A sample tweet could be:

> "FH Class @ FHL 2nite 7pm: Civil War Military Records, all welcome, wiki ref materials: https://wiki.familysearch.org/en/United_States_Civil_War%2C_1861_to_1865"

If an interested individual was in the area they could attend the class, additionally, the link provided could also help someone who is not able to attend but would like to learn about Civil War Military records.

Note the long URL above; if an individual does not have room for such a long URL in addition to the message, they can use one of the free sites to shrink the URL down to 20 or 25 characters. A couple of the more popular websites are *http://bit.ly* and *http://tinyurl.com*, either one of these websites will shrink the above link down considerable. Using TinyURL the above 72 character link was shrunk to 25 characters: http://tinyurl.com/2cm9sd9, while using Bit.ly it shrunk it down to 20 characters: http://bit.ly/eal5DK, reducing the number of characters in the message in order for the tweet to go out to those who are following.

Conferences are another great place to use

Twitter. No one individual can attend all the classes

they may want to, however, conferences will have a

group hashtag (#) so everyone can tweet while in

different classes and share the knowledge. The hashtag

for RootsTech is #rootstech. To follow multiple tweets

by a particular individual, by topics or a hashtag, one

can use a *Tweetdeck*, which is an online console with

the ability to watch five or six tweets at the same time.

Lastly, *Twitter* is great for taking polls, suppose you are trying to decide which scanner is the best for your genealogical needs, you could easily tweet your query and watch the answers that come back to aid you in selecting the best one for your needs.

Chapter 4

Blogs

In the early days of the internet, web sites were created by programmers and managed by web masters who were paid very well for their services. The everyday individual usually didn't have their own website; however some did venture forth and learn just how to create one. Most sites were government sites, commercial sites or non-profit sites due to the high costs of creating and maintaining an interesting static website.

New technology combined with open source code has brought about dynamic websites that adjust to the users' interests and searches along with personalization as well as the ability for individuals to create their own websites very easily. One of these types of websites is known as *Blogs.* Turning to

Wikipedia we find the following definition of a blog:

> A *blog* (a blend of the term web log) is a type of
> website or part of a website. Blogs are usually
> maintained by an individual with regular entries
> of commentary, descriptions of events, or other
> material such as graphics or video. Entries are
> commonly displayed in reverse-chronological
> order. *Blog* can also be used as a verb, meaning
> to maintain or add content to a blog.
>
> Most blogs are interactive, allowing visitors to
> leave comments and even message each other
> via widgets on the blogs and it is this
> interactivity that distinguishes them from other
> static websites.[11]

This interactivity provides a constant stream of

information to the reader and the blogger to the point

that blogs can be instructive, informative and even

educational. Those who contribute through comments

can provide additional and valuable details to the

_____

[11] "Blog - Wikipedia, the free encyclopedia." Wikipedia, the free
encyclopedia. http://en.wikipedia.org/wiki/Blog (accessed
January 7, 2011).

original blog entry. Adding photos and video and

improve the user experience tremendously.

Blogs create a reverse-chronological archive of

all posts so individuals can search the whole website,

including the archives, for information on a specific

topic. According to *Blogpulse*, as of January 6, 2011,

there are 153,051,152 total identified blogs.[12] Blogs

have become a new way to share and publish what use

to be only done through print or not done at all

because of cost.

Both authors have blogs that educate in

different ways. *DearMyrtle's Genealogy Blog* by Pat

Richley-Erickson provides up to date information on

the latest genealogical news as shown below for

---

[12] "BlogPulse." BlogPulse. http://www.blogpulse.com/ (accessed January 6, 2011).

January 6, 2011, it is located at

http://blog.dearmyrtle.com/2011/01/online-genealogy

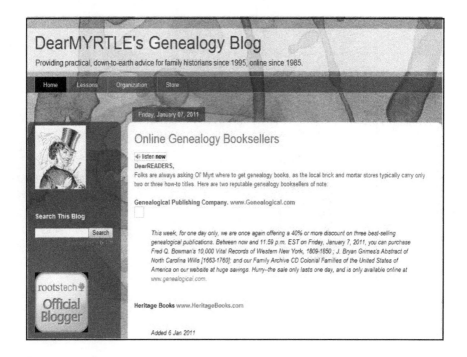

While, "Who will tell their stories" by Claire V.

Brisson-Banks, shares biographical stories of ancestors

along with a picture and a little history to share with

relatives all over the world. There is an invitation for

others who would like their ancestor featured on this

blog site to contact her and provide the necessary

information for a post. The site is located at

http://timelessgen.blogspot.com/

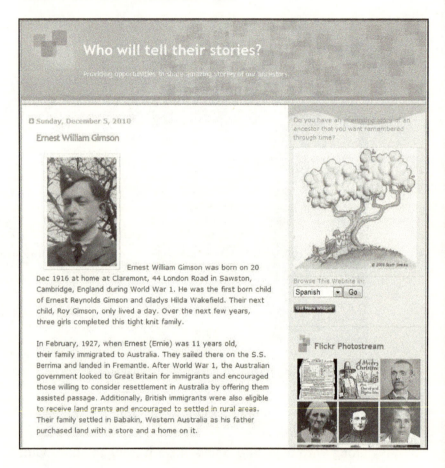

Blogs are a great resource for family historians and genealogists and their subjects are as varied as those who create them. The "no cost" through websites like *Blogger.com* and *WordPress.org* make it possible for anyone anywhere to use a little creativity and start a blog. Each site provides step by step directions along with video demonstrations making it very easy to create your own blog geared to a theme you feel is important to share with the world.

To find a list of available blogs for family history or genealogy, check out *Cyndislist.com* at http://www.cyndislist.com/blogs.htm, you just may locate a blog that can aid you in your research while also getting ideas on a topic to set one up for yourself. In addition, *Genealogy Blog Finder* can help you get more specific when seeking additional ideas or assistance with research. This site is located at http://blogfinder.genealogue.com/; it is worth noting that they have a 'What's New' section along with a section for those who frequent this site. Happy Blogging!

Chapter 5

Wikis

Mention the word *Wiki* and most individuals think of *Wikipedia.* This year is their 10th anniversary and has become a ready reference tool for many who need information quickly. In fact the actual word *wiki* is the Hawaiian term for "quick". The computing dictionary says it best as far as providing a great definition of a wiki

> Any collaborative website that users can easily modify via the web, typically without restriction. A wiki allows anyone, using a web browser, to edit, delete or modify content that has been placed on the site, including the work of other authors. This has been found to work surprisingly well since contributors tend to be more numerous and persistent than vandals and old versions of pages are always available. Text is entered using a simple mark-up language which is then rendered as HTML.[13]

---

[13] wiki. Dictionary.com. *The Free On-line Dictionary of Computing.* Denis Howe. http://dictionary.reference.com/browse/wiki (accessed: January 08, 2011).

Wikis involve communities of individuals that are connected by a specific topic, project or for building knowledge bases which is what *Wikipedia* has become. Another up and coming major Wiki is the *FamilySearch Research Wiki* which is being built by the genealogical community along with many of the Family History Library's staff. According to their website, "everyone knows something that can help someone else and they have 46, 307 resource pages as of January, 2011." [14]

This collaborative effort has produced amazing results for family history and genealogical researchers throughout the world. Starting with beta versions in October, 2007 and again in March, 2008 to its current

_____

[14]"Help: Wiki Overview." FamilySearch Research Wiki. https://wiki.familysearch.org/en/Help:Wiki_Overview (accessed January 8, 2011).

version is vital to the genealogical research community.

No two wikis are identical, in fact wikis are dynamic as users can log in and make changes to pages as they see fit. This is one of the major differences between blogs and wikis. Whereas blogs are the thoughts and opinions of one individual in the main content, a wikis' contents is the collaborative effort of countless numbers of individuals working together to provide valuable information to users everywhere.

As with blogs there are 'no cost' wiki software applications that one can use to create a wiki like *MediaWiki.org, PBwiki.com, TWiki.org,* and

Zoho.com/Wiki, of course there are many others but these are some of the more well know free applications. To locate addition wikis, use type in genealogical or family history wikis and enjoy the results.

According to their website, *WeRelate.org* is the largest genealogy wiki, their site contains contributed family trees of users of the site working together to build a 'unified family tree'. Just as in all other wikis, anyone can edit the information on an ancestor and

together collaborate on supporting documents.

Dick Eastman's *Encyclopedia of Genealogy* at

http://www.eogen.com is another great resource wiki

that provides free content created by the users and is

an online reference manual to aid researchers with

information on anything connected with genealogy.

Encyclopedia of Genealogy
An online reference manual created by you and others like you.

http://www.eogen.com

The *BiographicalWiki.com* was created by

Stephen D. Robison who saw the opportunity to allow

individuals to add stories about their ancestors and link

to supporting documents and data from within each

article. According to his site he has 5, 752 pages in his

database which remains free to access and search. This

is a great aid to fellow researchers.[15]

Wikis are being used for family projects,

cemetery transcriptions, reconstruction of a city by

creating historical pages for each of the towns and

villages and collaborative efforts throughout various

communities with the emphasis on "We are Smarter

than Me" which is taken from a book of the same title

by Barry Libert and John Spector. [16]

---

[15] "Main Page - Biographical Wiki." Main Page - Biographical Wiki.
http://www.biographicalwiki.com/index.php/Main_Page
(accessed January 9, 2011).

[16] Libert, Barry, and Jon Spector. We are smarter than me: how to
unleash the power of crowds in your business. Upper Saddle
River, N.J.: Wharton School Pub., 2008

Do you have a scattered family? You might consider building a family wiki and use it for genealogy both past and present and watch the success as it grows into a vibrant family community that will be enjoyed not only now but for generations.

WikiTree.com may be a good place to begin. Families can privately build their site while profiles exist in an interconnected worldwide family tree which encourages collaboration and connections with new found cousins.

Chapter 6

Forums

The art of collaboration has been evident in genealogical circles for years. This has been done through both (internet) forums and bulletin boards since the beginning of the internet in the 1990s. These internet communities have been a great way to share information, build a community, run a poll, get advice and zero in on any specific topic.

Webopedia provides a great definition of forums:

> An online discussion group. Online services and bulletin board services (BBS's) provide a variety of forums, in which participants with common interests can exchange open messages. Forums are sometimes called newsgroups (in the Internet world) or conferences. [17]

---

[17] "What is forum? - A Word Definition from the Webopedia Computer Dictionary." Webopedia: Online Computer Dictionary for Computer and Internet Terms and Definitions. http://www.webopedia.com/TERM/F/forum.html (accessed January 10, 2011).

This type of communication is called 'asynchronous' which means a single conversation where the individual waits for a reply as opposed to a chat where there is back and forth communication. Forum participants post a 'thread' which is usually a problem or situation where additional information is needed by the user, the greater the details the better the chance for a response. Anyone in this virtual community can respond at any time to this user's query or situation once they are registered to the forum. One does *not* have to be a registered member to browse the current or archived files in a forum for additional ideas and assistance in their research.

The various threads are archived for later reference. When a reply is posted, the user can receive an email notice that someone has responded to their query if they have set their preferences to receive email notices. If this is not done, an individual would have to remember to periodically check for any new postings. Like other online communities, genealogical forums are broken up by subjects and surnames to allow for easy searching.

The social side of forums is that individuals come together to help one another out regardless of physical locations. Forums were the forerunner to online networking. Over time these forums built their communities through participation, trust and responding to one another's problems whenever possible.

GenForum and *RootsWeb* are two of the more popular sites that have been on the internet for many years. When joining these well established communities the new individual can be confident that

50

if help is available they will receive it. In return, if the

new member is able to answer another's query it is

always a good idea to do so. It will build credibility and

in return others will be more willing to assist the new

member.

FamilySearch Forums began as a beta in 2007

with the intent according to the FamilySearch Labs

site, "Through forums anyone can ask questions about

FamilySearch product features, research techniques,

hints, tips or even about specific families in specific

locations."[18] A quick look at the actual site shows it

broken down by Localities, FamilySearch Support,

Historical Records Collections, FamilySearch Indexing,

---

[18] "Current Projects: Forums." FamilySearch Labs: Future Tools to
Dig Up the Past. https://labs.familysearch.org/ (accessed January
10, 2011).

New FamilySearch, FamilySearch Wiki, Family History

Center Support and Feedback and Help.

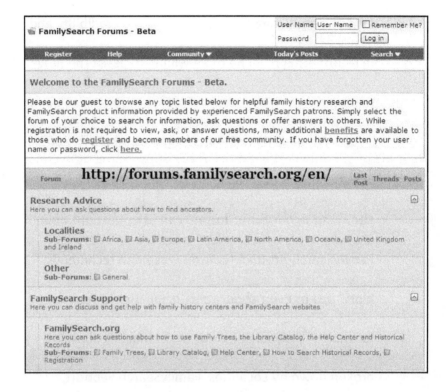

There are many more forums worth checking

out like *familytreecircles.com* and others that are

based on nationalities like the following:

- *"Italian Genealogy Online"* at

  http://tinyurl.com/4maebjg

- *African-Native American Genealogy* at
  http://www.afrigeneas.com/forume,
- *Armenian Genealogy Forum* at
  http://www.armeniangenealogy.org/forum
- *The Royal Irish Constabulary Forum* at
  http://irishconstabulary.com
- *Ireland County Forums* at
  http://www.cmcrp.net/forum
- *Genealogy.net-A European forum* at
  http://tinyurl.com/4kdyl5x
- *Jewish Forum* at http://genforum.genealogy

While there are many other forums available it takes

only a few clicks to check to see if there is a forum for a

specific area. Sign up for the one that is right for your

research needs and/or see someone else's question

that you can answer, working together can solve many

brick walls.

Chapter 7

Real Simple Syndication (RSS)

The internet is a plethora of web sites that can help anyone with anything. This creates the problem of trying to keep up with all the websites you normally would visit and keep track of any new web sites you may find interesting and worth spending time visiting. Information overload is everywhere, so how do individuals stay on top of this situation?

Real Simply Syndication (RSS) makes this task much simpler as users are able to subscribe to individual pages. So what is RSS? *Press feed* provides the following definition:

> RSS stands for Really Simple Syndication. Also called web feeds, RSS is a content delivery vehicle. It is the format used when you want to syndicate news and other web content. When it distributes the content it is called a feed. You

could think of RSS as your own personal wire service.[19]

When a website is updated with new information, it is sent to the subscriber providing constant updates without the subscriber having to log in and retrieve the new information. News stories, headlines, blogs, wikis, weather, technology updates, the latest information on anything can have a RSS feed. Individuals just need to look for this symbol somewhere on the website, click it and subscribe to that feed.

RSS

The feed icon used in several browsers
Filename extension   .rss, .xml

http://en.wikipedia.org/wiki/Rss_feeds

[19] "RSS Feeds Definition | RSS Feed Tutorial and Basics : PRESSfeed." Social Media Newsroom | Pressfeed. http://www.press-feed.com/howitworks/rss_tutorial.php (accessed January 12, 2011).

Once the user signs up for an RSS feed it will be necessary to choose a format to receive this information which is known as a feed reader. The feed reader aggregates the updates to look like any other web page and places them all on a webpage, the results for the user is to just click on the news item of interest and it opens up the new information.

Genealogists of all levels are always looking for ways to get the latest information on a particular subject matter as well as many other websites of interest. If the above symbol is on the website of interest subscribing requires only a few clicks. Favorite blogs, wikis, family history societies, conference updates as well as new products are just some of the possible categories for using RSS feeds.

There are a number of ways to subscribe to RSS feeds but the easiest way is to set up an *iGoogle* page.

A click on the actual words will take you to the

beginning of creating a home page of RSS feeds

through the use of adding gadgets, which are just small

applications, to sites of interest by topic or locality.

Another way to keep up with websites, blogs

and wikis is to use *Google Reader*; which is a feed

reader. It monitors all these sites for you and can be

accessed from any computer with an internet

connection.

Another way to subscribe to an RSS feed is

through your internet browser. This service is available

in Internet Explorer (IE) 7 and IE8. With the browser open simply click your *Favorites* menu and select the *Feeds* tab, click "Add to Favorites Bar" down arrow and the option to *Subscribe to this feed* becomes available if this site has RSS feeds available.

In addition to the *Favorites* menu, the symbol becomes available in the top to click and subscribe with IE8:

http://www.archives.gov

If Mozilla Firefox is the internet browser of

choice, go to *Bookmarks,* if there is no feed available it

will be grayed out, if available a click will allow the

subscription to take place.

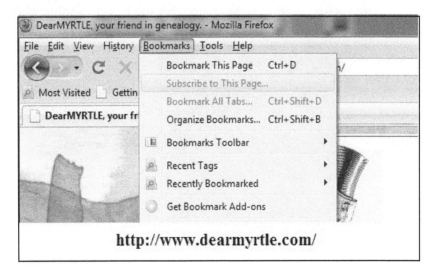

http://www.dearmyrtle.com/

Various email programs also allow users to subscribe to RSS feeds that arrive along with regular email, *Outlook, Mozilla Thunderbird, Windows Live Mail* and *Opera* are a few free email programs that include this convenient feature.

Regardless of which method is chosen to subscribe to the different websites available, the process has been greatly simplified in the last few years. Technology has provided another great resource to those wanting to keep up with the latest in their field.

Chapter 8

Social Bookmarking

Saving time by bookmarking websites has been extremely helpful for most over the years as one of the ways to staying organized with online activities. The continued growth of new information relating to work, school or individual interests on the internet has created for most a very long list of bookmarked websites.

The introduction of social bookmarking adds a new perspective that allows anyone to share their bookmarks in an easy way with no limits to the number of favorite websites. *FirstPageSage* provides a great definition of this great resource:

> Social bookmarking is the practice of locating, organizing, storing and sharing bookmarks of web pages usually facilitated by a web hosting service such as *Digg*, *Del.icio.us*, *Reddit*, and *StumbleUpon*. Users tag webpages by assigning metadata (keywords) that indicates the content of the

particular website and providing a link to it. The webpages are then collated in a list or web feed, making it easily accessible to users searching for bookmarks related to their interest. Social bookmarking is a valuable way of sharing resources over the Internet and creating instant awareness of a particular website.[20]

It is well known that no one person can do it all and this is where social media plays a big role. By sharing favorite websites with other users the possibility of being exposed to a new resource is made possible. Adding tags to each website helps to build a community catalog that everyone can use to locate new websites.

Once an account is set up, the user can upload their bookmarks/favorite sites; this establishes their personal list of bookmarks. Sharing, adding tags or

---

[20] Bailyn, Evan. "Definition ofSocial Bookmarking – Social Media and SEO Glossary - First Page Sage." First Page Sage | Expert Google Optimization and Social Media Marketing. http://firstpagesage.com/social-bookmarking (accessed January 15, 2011).

deleting a specific website can be done at this level.
Once the sharing icon or box has been indicated it is
automatically added to whole collection of websites by
all users, it is that simple.

Delicious.com is known to have the largest
collection of bookmarks in the universe and was the
first web-based social bookmarking system. It was
established by Joshua Schachter in 2003 and acquired
by *Yahoo* in 2005. Today, various statistics mention
subscribers in the millions which would account for
such a large collection.

Networking comes naturally to genealogists as they constantly reach out to one another whenever possible. Social bookmarking is a powerful way to enhance this networking as individuals share their websites with everyone. Brick wall situations could be solved if a new, previously unknown website held the answer and was discovered through this type sharing.

The short list provided in the definition is definitely a start to choosing one to join or if the thought of reaching out more individuals appeals join them all as each one reaches different audiences. To help users decide, the authors turn to *Alexa.com* which is a web information company that provides statistics on websites along with a brief history.

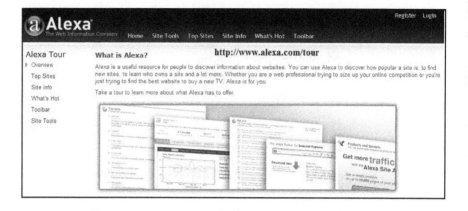

Regardless of which social bookmarking website is chosen, the first step will be to export the bookmarks that are currently residing on the personal computer used daily. Each site provides step by step directions, but a review here can help to familiarize a user with the terminology used in their directions.

Both *IE* and *Firefox* have export and import features that are simple to follow, once you go through the steps the final trick will be to write down the name of the bookmark file and its location on the PC. Once that is known it will be much easier to upload the file to the chosen bookmarking website.

To create the file in *IE*, click on "File" and "Export" which will bring up a simple dialog box which allows the individual to click through each instruction with the default end result being a file called **bookmark.htm** saved in the document folder. As with all save commands, the user can name the file something different and save it in a different place.

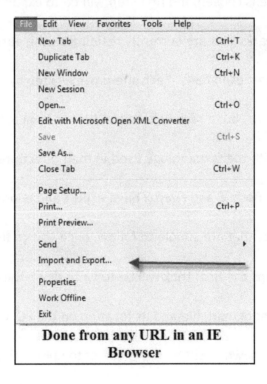

File	Edit	View	Favorites	Tools	Help	
New Tab						Ctrl+T
Duplicate Tab						Ctrl+K
New Window						Ctrl+N
New Session						
Open...						Ctrl+O
Edit with Microsoft Open XML Converter						
Save						Ctrl+S
Save As...						
Close Tab						Ctrl+W
Page Setup...						
Print...						Ctrl+P
Print Preview...						
Send						▶
Import and Export...						
Properties						
Work Offline						
Exit						

Done from any URL in an IE Browser

If Firefox is the browser of choice the steps are a little different. Click on the "Bookmarks" up at the very top between "History" and "Tools", from the dropdown menu, click on "Organize Bookmarks" if in Firefox 3.6.2. The import feature is at the very top of the window that pops open, once there, click the "Import and Backup" and in the dropdown menu click Export HTML. This action pops up a save window which allows the individual to choose the name of the file and its location.

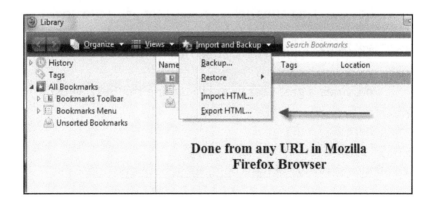

Done from any URL in Mozilla Firefox Browser

To show the additional value to these sites, the
author typed in *'Genealogy'*, *'Family History'*,
'Ancestors', and *"Immigration"* to see the 'hits' results
available to a researcher.

Social Site	Genealogy	Family History	Ancestors	Immigration
Delicious	101,406	24,064	5498	124,703
Digg	2444	9037	6724	61.696
Reddit	260	240	490	6200
StumbleUpon*	12,901	19,931	33,454	76,197

*Note that *StumbleUpon.com* only allows searchers
once the individual has signed up to be part of the
community. Any and all of the above social
bookmarking sites holds promise for any genealogist.
There are many other similar websites; *Squidoo.com*
provides a great list to aid in picking the best website
here
http://www.squidoo.com/socialbookmarkingsites.

Take advantage of their RSS feed and keep up with the

latest news concerning social bookmarking.

Chapter 9

Sharing Digital Images

"A picture is worth a thousand words" is said to have originated from a different individuals. In December, 1921, Frederick R. Barnard entitled a graphics article, *"One look is worth a thousand words"*, in *Printer's Ink*. The article about the phrase goes on to say that who actually linked up 'picture' with 'worth ten thousand words' is unknown but that the phrase is American in origin.[21]

Regardless, it is true that pictures add so much to everything including genealogical and family history research. The joy one has when locating a picture of an ancestor is immense and often beyond words in

---

[21] "A picture is worth a thousand words." The meanings and origins of sayings and phrases.
http://www.phrases.org.uk/meanings/a-picture-is-worth-a-thousand-words.html (accessed January 16, 2011).

description of their importance. Taking the next step and sharing those pictures with family, friends and the community takes research to a new level as distance cousins find one another by connecting family members through pictures.

Before cameras individuals relied on hand drawings throughout history to provide insights into everything connected with history. The first permanent photograph was a 'daguerreotype' made in 1826 by Joseph Nicephore Niepce while the first color photograph was made by James Clerk Maxwell, a Scottish physicist and Thomas Sutton, an English inventor in 1861.[22]

Perhaps the driving force behind this invention was the constant need to make a record of human

---

[22] "Camera - Wikipedia, the free encyclopedia." Wikipedia, the free encyclopedia. http://en.wikipedia.org/wiki/Camera (accessed January 16, 2011).

events not only in text but in pictures. The introduction of digital images in combination with the advances in technology and internet applications has changed everything and made it possible to learn more and more about one's ancestors from anywhere in the world. To genealogists and family historians pictures bring life to their ancestral stories.

The number of ways to share photos continues to grow as time goes on. Stepping away from snail mail one goes to email attachments. Photos can be part of a regular website, a blog, a wiki, a social networking website or photo sharing websites like *Flickr, Picasa, Shutterfly, Photobucket,* and *Snapfish.* The services provided by these websites are tremendous. If photos are scanned and uploaded it is a way of preserving precious memories which often cannot be replaced in case of disasters. *FirstPageSage* provides the following

definition of photo sharing sites:

> Photo sharing refers to the act of posting and
> sharing digital photos online for private or public
> consumption. This is usually done through
> photosharing websites who allow users to post,
> edit, manage and share images with online
> communities and through email. Some popular
> photo-sharing sites are Flickr, Picasa and
> Photobucket. Another form of photo sharing online
> is by posting photos on a blog or social networking
> site.[23]

Sharing digital photos is a fairly simple process.

The memory card the photos are stored on can be

loaded into a PC and uploaded to a file folder. Once

the pictures are copied to the hard drive of a PC, it is a

matter of choosing the website to upload them too.

Just as in previous programs, each of the websites

listed above have different methods of sharing photos.

----

[23] Bailyn, Evan. "Definition ofPhoto Sharing – Social Media and
SEO Glossary - First Page Sage." First Page Sage | Expert Google
Optimization and Social Media Marketing.
http://firstpagesage.com/photo-sharing (accessed January 16,
2011).

Once the website is chosen, it is a matter of creating an account, uploading the photos and deciding through preferences whether the photos will be shared with the public, family and friends or kept totally private and only shared through personal invitations.

If the images are made public, the owner needs to decide whether others can share them through a Creative Commons License ⓒⓒ which has four types of licenses as described in *Flickr*:

1) ⓘ**Attribution**: You let others copy, distribute, display, and perform your copyrighted work – and derivative works based upon it – but only if they give you credit.

2) 🅢 **Noncommercial**: You let others copy, distribute, display, and perform your work – and derivative works based upon it – but for noncommercial purposes only.

3) ⊜ **No Derivative Works**: You let others copy,

distribute, display, and perform only verbatim

copies of your work, not derivative works based

upon it.

4) ⊚ **Share Alike means**: You allow others to

distribute derivative works only under a license

identical to the license that governs your

work.[24]

[24] "Flickr: Creative Commons." Welcome to Flickr - Photo Sharing.
http://www.flickr.com/creativecommons/ (accessed January 16,
2011).

Each of the websites suggested have a similar set up and the real decision becomes what photos will be shared? Who will I shall them with? Can these pictures help fellow genealogists also looking for ancestral photos? The list is endless as to the possibilities and the opportunity to discover new cousins.

Photos that reside in a makeshift container from years' past require the extra step of scanning to a hard drive. Many times when a loved one passes on their photos are either given to one individual or passed around to various descendants. Either way the best thing that can be done with all types of photos is to scan them to a hard drive and preserve the originals in a safe environment.

Determining the type of scanner is made easier with a little bit of knowledge in choosing which kind to use for your precious photos. According to

Consumersearch.com there are a few things to be

mindful of:

1) Flatbed configurations are easier to use for the

   widest range of scanning

2) The higher the resolution the better, especially

   for detailed photo jobs or for enlargements

3) Nearly all scanners are equipped with 48-bit

   color depth

4) Included software is standard, so look for a

   good package

5) If you want to convert scanned text into an

   editable document, you need OCR software[25]

---

[25] "Important Scanner Features - What to Look For." Product Reviews and Reports - ConsumerSearch.com. http://www.consumersearch.com/scanner-reviews/important-features (accessed January 16, 2011).

Additionally it is always wise to ask others who have scanned their photos what kind of scanner they are using. The combination of their answers and the above information should provide you with all you need to choose the best scanner for digitizing your precious memories!

Once the photos are digitized the procedure to upload them is the same as if they were originally digital photos. Be sure to label your pictures and save them with file names that help identify them. This will make the job easier when organizing photos on your personal computer.

Three more websites are worth pointing out that also are great help to genealogists and family historians; *FindaGrave.com, DeadFred.com* and *Ancestry.com.* Each of these sites has a different focus. *FindaGrave.com* is self descriptive and has become a great aid in locating family information from others

who have upload photos of ancestral burial locations.

Here is one of the authors' contributions that resulted

in contact with an unknown relative;

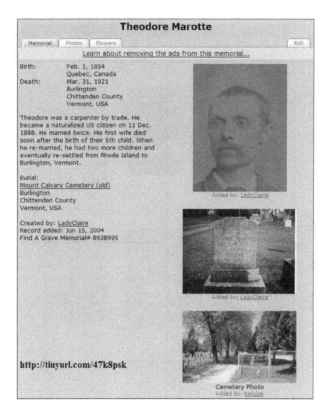

DeadFred.com is another website which strives

to assist those who have photos of family members

with no names as well as another place to save photos.

Searching through photos with no names can be

conducted by place, time period, photographer and

photo type. A simple search of photos from the USA

between the years 1835-1850 provided these results:

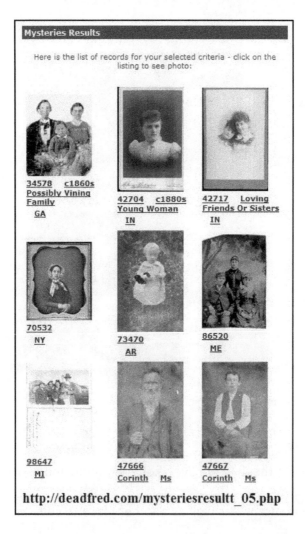

This website also has searches by surnames and keyword searches. This website has brought together 1,817 individuals with photos of loved ones. It is a definite aid to anyone looking for photos of loved ones. To date there are 17, 348 surnames and 102,551 photos to check for a relative at http://www.deadfred.com.

Ancestry.com has a section of their website dedicated to family photos also. Once you begin a search for an individual, 'Pictures' is in the drop down list of results to check in continuing the search.

▼ All Categories	
Census & Voter Lists	5,000+
Birth, Marriage & Death	5,000+
Military	764
Immigration & Travel	1,606
Newspapers & Publications	148
Pictures	153
Stories, Memories & Histories	148
Schools, Directories & Church Histories	5,000+
Tax, Criminal, Land & Wills	13
Reference, Dictionaries & Almanacs	67
Family Trees	5,000+

http://ancestry.com

Once clicked the category breaks further down to *Public Member Photos & Scanned Documents*, it is here that an unknown family photo could be discovered! As more photos are uploaded to these and other websites, the chance of locating lost or unknown photos increases. As more and more individuals share their photos this community will continue to grow and find new families they belong too.

Chapter 10

Sharing Video Files

The 1950s brought with it the ability to create family home movies with a Kodak 8 mm camera and share them with the film projector. While the cost was high, there were many families that saved and were able to create these priceless gems. Those who have these films are able to recall a time long past and enjoy the visualization of their ancestors.

The 1980s introduced video recording which allowed even greater movie making ability to families around the world. Today short movies can be taken with a cell phone or digital cameras and those early home movies can be upgraded into digital format to preserve them for future generations. *Pcmag.com* provides us with a great definition of video sharing sites:

A Web site that lets people upload and share their video clips with the public at large or to invited guests. Acquired by Google in 2006, YouTube became the most popular video sharing site on the Web. See YouTube, Vimeo, Flip Video and Google Apps. See also document sharing site.[26]

Web 1.0 was a time of 'static' websites; however, videos were added to make these websites enjoyable for individuals who visited them. Family websites with family movies were created as well as non-commercial and commercial websites. With the help of the *Internet Archives' Way Back Machine*, individuals can view a website from its origins if they provide the website address.

[26] "PCMAG.COM: Encyclopedia: video sharing site." PCMAG.COM Encyclopedia.
www.pcmag.com/encyclopedia_term/0,2542,t=video+sharing+site&i=57378,00.asp (accessed January 16, 2011).

The combination of technological advances and new applications brought about the ability for individuals to create, upload, share and view videos in an online environment. To fill this need *YouTube.com* was founded in 2005 by Chad Hurley, Steve Chen and Jawed Karim with the vision of providing everyone a video voice as stated in their *Frequently Asked Questions* section.[27]

YouTube.com provides a great resource to individuals throughout the world and a search for "families" will result in quite a listing of family videos available to watch. In addition to posting the video on *YouTube*, individuals can reference these same videos in blogs, wikis, various social networks as well as

---

[27] " YouTube-Broadcast Yourself. ." YouTube-Broadcast Yourself. . http://www.youtube.com/t/faq (accessed January 16, 2011).

emailing the web address known as a *Uniform Resource Locator* (URL) to their friends and family.

These new resources have made recording and sharing oral histories a reality. In addition to oral histories on *YouTube.com,* there are other websites dedicated to making video oral histories available to the world. Some of these histories can be located by subject matter, ethnicity, time period or events in history.

The University of Southern California (USC) has a website dedicated to the Shoah Foundation Institute where there are over 52,000 video testimonies of Holocaust survivors and additional witnesses. According to their website they encourage universities, museums and other institutions to help create the Visual History Archive and make it available for the world so that many people can conduct their research.[28]

The *American Historical Association* constantly publishes online audio and video oral histories. The section shown below would be helpful to individuals who had family members involved in the military operations covered below.

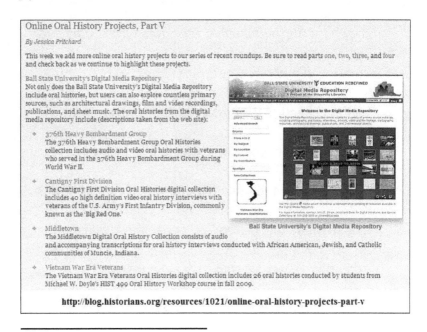

---

[28] "Home | USC Shoah Foundation Institute." *USC College of Letters, Arts & Sciences*. N.p., n.d. Web. 16 Jan. 2011. <http://college.usc.edu/vhi/>.

There are many other types of videos available to aid researchers depending on their need. Creating a video and uploading it has become as simple as sharing files by email. *DropShots.com* allows for families to create an account, upload videos and photos and share them with families and friends.

There are many options to aid researchers as they hunt for their illusive ancestors who could have created an audio or video recording that is part of a bigger collection. The *Internet Archive* has a *Movie Archive* section where it is possible to locate historical information in their section entitled *Then and Now*. A search on 'family history' or 'genealogy' will provide additional materials that may aid a researcher.

Once a video hosting website is chosen follow their directions for uploading videos by first creating an account and the video. Sharing genealogical and family history videos can bring new relatives and

information that could help solve a brick wall problem

or the solution is there waiting to be discovered.

Internet Archive Blogs

Home   About

← Eels as party favors?   The Fourth Generation Petabox →

Then and Now

Posted on July 22, 2010 by internetarchive

With the continued difficulties in the economy and the comparison often heard to the Great Depression I thought I'd search the Archive for some perspective. While unquestionably there was hardship and suffering, I was heartened to see footage from two places that show daily life.

http://blog.archive.org/2010/07/22/2312/

Chapter 11

Podcasts and Vodcasts

Staying on top of the latest new genealogical

and family history research tools available can be a

daunting task if one has to sit to watch everything.

Quickly skimming a new book is helpful especially if the

book is quickly available, however, there are times

when stopping to read a book can be impossible.

Taking a lead from audio books are podcasts and

vodcasts.

808Talk provides the definitions of podcasting
and vodcasting:

Podcasting

"A digital recording of a radio broadcast or similar
program, made available on the Internet for
downloading to a personal audio player."

Vodcasting

"Video podcast (sometimes shortened to vidcast or
vodcast) is a term used for the online delivery of

video on demand video clip content via Atom or RSS enclosures."[29]

Over time stories have been told of how before television families use to gather around the radio and listen to a specific radio show or the news. In a similar fashion, podcasts aid their listeners by providing vital information by discussing a particular subject or interviewing an expert in a research area that may provide enough information to solve a research problem.

Conference lectures and presentations can also be put into a podcast environment allowing for additional training long after the conference is done.

_____

[29] "What Is Podcasting/Vodcasting? | 808Talk.com | 808Talk Hawaii." 808Talk Hawaii: Podcast/Vodcast/Blog/News - Sharing Aloha With The World - ハワイ - Hawaii Vacations, News, Views, Travel Tips, Events, Music and Culture Through Online Radio Blogging. http://www.808talk.com/what-is-podcasting/ (accessed January 17, 2011).

The convenience of a podcast is the ability to download the broadcast to an MP3 player or similar device that handles MP3s, attach earphones and listen while doing other necessary things. Individuals are able to increase their knowledge while still working on other tasks that need to be handled on a daily basis.

While podcasts are downloadable 'audio' files, vodcasts are downloadable video files which can be viewed on portable video players (PVP). Vodcasts are distributed as a file or as a video stream allowing the user to view at a convenient time. Today's smart phones, iPods, and other devices that support both audio and video will be sufficient to take advantage of these great resources.

Once the decision to download a podcast or a vodcast is made, a user has to locate a client where these types of files are available. The most well known client is *iTunes* which is a software-based media store owned and operated by Apple, Inc. While the convenience of listening and/or watching on a portable device is the main thrust behind *iTunes*, downloading the software to a PC allows for watching and listening on the PC.

Visiting the *iTunes* Store is done by going to http://www.apple.com/itunes/ and clicking on the 'Download iTunes' blue button on the upper right hand side of the website. This brings you to the following screen.

Once the 'Download Now' button is pushed the program can be installed to a PC or a Mac. The next step is locating the audio and/or video files of interest. If you are new to *iTunes* you will have to create an account. Once that is done a simple login will bring you to the point of locating files of interest.

On the left hand side under 'Library' select 'iTunes Store', next type in 'genealogy' in the search box located in the upper right hand corner. Once the search is complete, scroll down to 'Podcasts' where a small list is displayed, clicking on the 'view all' brings up the following:

Most of the available podcasts and vodcasts are free to subscribe to. Once the 'subscribe' button is clicked, the podcasts are automatically downloaded to the PC and available relatively quickly. It is worth noting that if there is another interest, the same steps can be completed for that additional interest or topic.

Additional podcasts and vodcasts can be located through using an internet browser and typing in 'genealogy podcasts', 'genealogy vodcasts', 'family history podcasts', or family history vodcasts'. There are many available from the websites of those who produce them and not available through *iTunes.* Try different search terms like 'roots podcasts' and 'FamilySearch podcasts', the results listing may have just what is needed to help along the research trail.

Chapter 12

E-Learning and Online Classes

Education is the key to improved research and outcomes. The opportunities to attain this knowledge have increased substantially with the aid of new technology combined with internet access. Add the component of convenience and this new method of education becomes a win-win combination for those providing the education and those receiving the new knowledge.

About E-Learning provides this definition from *The American Society for Training and Development*:

> The American Society for Training and Development (ASTD) defines e-learning as a broad set of applications and processes which include web-based learning, computer-based learning, virtual classrooms, and digital. Much of this is delivered via the Internet, intranets, audio- and videotape, satellite broadcast, interactive TV, and CD-ROM. The definition of e-learning varies depending on the organization and how it is used but basically it is

involves electronic means of communication, education, and training.[30]

The type of communications between the teacher and student will depend on the type of e-learning course being taken. Online interactions are always at the mercy of the internet connection which can cause difficulty when least expected. Some classroom situations are set up in a chat room with audio for the instructor and participants along with the video of a PowerPoint presentation.

Live classes can also be broadcast where the student logs in and interacts with the whole class including the instructor; these are called 'Distance

---

[30] "Definition of e-learning | E-learning definition | Define e learning." *About e-Learning | Online Degrees | Online Colleges | Online Distance Education*. N.p., n.d. Web. 17 Jan. 2011. <http://www.about-elearning.com/definition-of-e-learning.html>.

Learning' through remote classroom instruction (RCI) and are available in many locations.

Other types of online classes are done through teleconferencing and webinars which go a long way in creating a virtual classroom environment. Each of these methods has different advantages and provides the opportunity for the participants to respond to the topics and the others in the classroom.

Various groups and individuals have created and placed instructional videos online to help people who wish to learn anything from a foreign language to research skills and so much more on their own time schedule. These types of videos can be found in many different locations besides *YouTube.com* although that is a good place to begin if only to see what is available for viewing.

Using *YouTube.com* as a starting point, an

individual might just type in the word 'genealogy

research' or 'family history' to see what is available.

The results are amazing as the number of videos

available is in the thousands.

Search results for **genealogy research**
About **1,110** results

Search options

Genealogy Search Basics
The first of 17 how-to video lessons from the "5 Minute Genealogy" course (on a set of two CDs). Remember that YouTube really cuts the quality of ...
by 5minutegenealogy 3 years ago **13,503 views**
5:05

Using Google News Timeline for **Genealogy** & Family History
Google News Timeline is an ideal tool for family historians who want to further their genealogy research. Lisa Louise Cooke, host of the popular ...
by GenealogyGems 1 year ago **13,736 views**
9:06

Ancestry Library Edition **Genealogy Research** in 2 Minutes
Ancestry Library Edition, distributed exclusively by ProQuest and powered by Ancestry.com, delivers over 4 billion records in census data, vital ...
by timproquest 10 months ago **1,513 views**
1:22

http://www.youtube.com/results?
search_query=genealogy+research&aq=f

Search results for **family history research**
About 3,330 results

Search options

Genealogy #01: Beginning Your **Family** Tree
The basics of genealogy beginning with downloading free forms, putting your data into genealogy programs, looking up information on the web, etc ...
by freetutorials 2 years ago **20,707 views**
9:55

Beginning **Family History Research** by The Nosey Genealogist
www.NoseyGenealogist.com The web has made Beginning Family History Research to find our ancestors so much easier to do. As more and more data ...
by NoseyGenealogist 1 year ago **605 views**
8:09

Get Original Genealogy and **Family History** Records with FamilySearch New Record **Search** Pilot site
You've got to try this. You may have been to the FamilySearch site before, but what they are working on is truly wonderful. I'm talking about ...
by GenealogyGuy 2 years ago **29,000 views**
6:45

http://www.youtube.com/results?
search_query=family+history+research&aq=f

Any of these videos along with the additional 5,000

plus will provide information that may be helpful in

conducting research. As with all knowledge there are

different levels to consider when adding to one's

knowledge base on any given topic and genealogical

research is no different.

There are organizations that specialize in Family

History and Genealogical research and preservation.

They are located throughout the world and known as 'Genealogical Organizations', 'Family History Societies', 'Genealogical Institutions',' National, Regional, State and local Archives', 'Family History Library and Centers', as well as small local groups whose main focus is to preserve the heritage of their area.

Over time many of these groups have classes on how to use their facilities as well as sponsor conferences that are held on an annual basis. Technology has made it possible for many of these groups to develop online training through videos combined with syllabus materials that can be printed and used along with the instructional video. Their success is varied, however, more and more of them are made available over time. The next few clips are from various locations where one will be able to locate genealogical and/or family history research guidance.

FamilySearch provides over a hundred different research courses to aid a researcher with more being added every month:

This series of research courses includes videos done by the Accredited Genealogical (AG) staff at the Family History Library, members of the Association of Professional Genealogists (APG), Certified Genealogists (CG), the Midwest Genealogical Center staff, the

Library of Congress staff, and other guest lecturers who are experts in this field.

The selection covers the United States, England, Germany, Ireland, Poland, New Zealand, Italy, Mexico, Russia and valuable topics like *Reading Handwritten Records, Descendancy Research, Research Principals and Tools* and so much more, visit the site at thttps://learning.familysearch.org/researchcourses.

Ancestry.com has a 'Learning Center' that has videos, webinars, tutorials, their magazine, and archives from past newsletters.

There are over forty different webinar

presentations to choose with topics like 'Common

Surnames: Ways to Identify Your Ancestors in a

Crowd', 'Coming to America: Finding Your Immigrant

Ancestors', 'Finding Females in Your Family Tree' and

so many more. Clicking on the link that says 'Webinars:

Online Seminars' will take you to their extensive list.

Online classes and courses are also available at

the following locations:

New England Historical Genealogical Society	http://tinyurl.com/4u424um
FamilyTree University	http://tinyurl.com/4zp7t58
Genealogy.com	http://tinyurl.com/4s95vkv
National Genealogical Society	http://tinyurl.com/4ommknd
National Institute for Genealogical Studies	http://tinyurl.com/4zc47f4
Pharos Tutors: Genealogy Courses Online	http://www.pharostutors.com/

While there are many other classes available

online, this is a small sample of what is offered through

E-learning. To keep up with this growing list, check out

Cyndislist.com at

http://www.cyndislist.com/educate.htm#Online. In

addition to the above listings, you will find home study

courses, credentialing courses and new resource

methods. Each class or course will bring new

information, knowledge, and research tips that can help with anyone's genealogical research endeavors.

The last area to discuss in connection with online instruction is *SecondLife*. *SecondLife* is a virtual world where avatars, representing live individuals, move around and function in an environment that contains other avatars, buildings, shops, schools, libraries and all the same kinds of things anyone would find in the live world.

Just as in the current world, there are genealogical classes held in various organizations represented in this virtual reality. One's avatar would attend the class, ask questions and come away having learned what was taught by the instructor. The following are some of the classes available in *SecondLife* through the *Union of Genealogy Groups* (UGG):

Destination	Meeting Times are in Second Life Times (SL)
Afterchillis Conference Room	Wednesdays at 6pm SL time
Danish Rots	By appointment hosted by Charlotta Jenkins
Family History Center	Sundays at 5:15pm SL time hosted by Clarise Beaumont
First Life Ancestry & Genealogy Center	Mondays at 5:15pm SL time hosted by Barbara Collazo and Constantine Kyomoon
Genealogy Research Center on Infolsland	3rd Wednesdays, 6pm SL time
Just Genealogy	Tuesdays at 6 pm SL time at the fire pit
The GenealogySource	Irish & Celtic Family History hosted by Jaylynn Sinatra

Find the teleport links by typing in the

destinations listed above, visit and meet others who

are willing to share their expertise in a totally new

environment. While there is a bit of a learning curve

with *SecondLife*, everyone is there to help one another

out as in real life.

Make new friends and learn new technologies

that will help to carry you into the next new reality

SecondLife.com. Both authors are involved in teaching classes in *SecondLife.*

Family History Centre @ AoA, Adam ondi Ahman - General

Chapter 13

Social Networking and Online Communities

Networking among genealogists has been going on for as long as there have been genealogists who are searching for their own ancestors or a client's ancestors. Adding a layer of internet connections through *Social Networking* was inevitable because of the enhanced ways of connecting with other individuals who may be related or researching similar family names.

Jed Segal provides a detailed explanation of Social Networking:

> Social networking is defined as the grouping of individuals together into to specific groups, often like a small community or a neighborhood. Although social networking is possible in person, especially in schools or in the workplace, it is most popular online. This is because unlike most high schools, colleges, or workplaces, the internet is filled with millions, if not more, of individuals who are looking to meet other internet users and develop friendships.

When it comes to social networking online, websites are used. These websites are known as social networking websites. Social networking websites are, in a way, like an online community of internet users. Depending on the social networking website in question, many of these online community members share a common bond, whether that bond is hobbies, religion, or politics. Once you are granted access to a social networking website you can begin to socialize. This socialization may include reading the profiles or profile pages of other members or even contacting them.

There are key phrases in the definition above that makes social networking a great resource tool for genealogists and family historians throughout the world. The main one is *"like a small community..."* combined with *"the internet is filled with millions...of individuals..."* Where else can an individual get the friendly home-type atmosphere that is found in small communities but on the level of reaching out to millions of people at the same time?

Individuals enjoy being around other people who share a common interests. One of the great benefits to social networking is the ability to meet new

people who may even share a legitimate relationship

which is discovered through email exchanges of

information done right on the social networking

service.

New cousins and friends can be from anywhere

in the world and often can provide new genealogical

data that would be otherwise unavailable. While

pictures can be uploaded and shared in most of these

virtual environments, documents can be emailed

separate if necessary.

In addition to locating new friends and/or

relations, these sites can also help locate friends and

relatives from the past where contact has been lost

over the years. Genealogists are wonderful at

providing research tips, encouraging others in their

research pursuits and gladly share about upcoming

events.

While there are many social networking

websites, *Facebook* and *GenealogyWise* are

spotlighted here as great resources for guidance as

well as locating new family members. Signing up for

each of these services is relatively simple. Go to their

websites:

Follow their directions for creating an account.

Once that is done, take time to look around and see

what others have done in each of the different

networks. Each network has different methods for

inviting others to join the same network. Just as a new person in a new area, it takes time to feel comfortable; however, the way to do that is to spend a little bit of time each day to do just that while linking up with friends and family while also meeting new friends and previously unknown family members.

It is worth pointing out that like all communities whether online or in person, privacy issues could be a reason individuals do not participate in social networking. There have been many articles written on how to maintain one's privacy through preference settings; it is wise to take the time to learn how to set the privacy levels of any social network. These can usually be located by searching in an internet browser with the words 'how to set privacy settings in *Facebook*" or any other social network. The results will be step by step guides to make the correct settings.

Adding friends and family to a network is where connections are often made with unknown relatives as has happened with the authors and others who have shared their stories either online or at various conferences in person.

In each case, an unknown or new family member sends either an email or asks to be a 'friend' or the new member reaches out to someone they think could be related. Once either contact is established, questions can be made to each privately and verification of a legitimate relationship can take place complimented with the exchange of photos and genealogical information.

In the screen shot below, genealogical information was exchanged with a new found relative about William Wakefield privately:

Photos were exchanged and ancestral lines were extended another generation which open the doors to further research and additional lines. This has happened multiple times and continues to happen more and more frequently.

GenealogyWise is a little different in that there are groups to join where genealogical information can be exchanged with other members who may end up being related. One of nice things about this networking website is the ability to tie in other social applications like *Flickr, Blogger.com*, and *Twitter*. Chat groups can be set up for discussions and participation in forums is encouraged.

The genealogical search engine is *World Vital Records* which boasts a collection of over 3.6 Billion Ancestral Genealogical records. Conducting a search will show you the results available, however, to see those results an individual would have to join their database service.

Other social networking and online communities of interest would be *Geni.com, GenesReunited.com, MyHeritage.com, WeRelate.com, AncestralSpace.com, FamilyLink.com, Arcalife.com* and many others.

Each of the above communities offers much for the genealogist. These websites act like an intermediary between the researcher and the information. Once an individual has joined, they upload a Gedcom* file of their data making sure that no information on living individuals is included in the upload.

*A Gedcom file is created with the aid of a genealogical database management program. It is an acronym for Genealogical Data COMmunication. Each program has a method of creating this file and allows for a way to remove information of living individuals that reside in a database. It is this file that is used in communicating through these online communities. The main five software packages are Ancestral Quest, Family Tree Maker, Legacy, Personal Ancestral File, and RootsMagic. Each of these software programs will manage genealogical data and create a Gedcom file suitable for sharing online.

A researcher looks on their website and locates a match, an email is sent to the holder of the information letting them know someone wishes to communicate because of a pending relation and asks for permission to view your data. Through this website, hundreds of names and photos have been added to this author's database after verifying them through proper documentation. The message center helps by identifying the connections by the relation.

Relation	Compose Message	Access to their tree	Access to your tree
Robert Gimson	✓	✓ View	✓ Stop
William Gimson	✓	✓ View	✓ Stop
William Gimson	✓	✗ Request	✓ Stop
Bertram Frost	✓	✓ View	✓ Stop
Jane Lockhart	✓	✓ View	✓ Stop

Genesreunited.com has also added historical records since they began their networking website in

2003. A search beyond an index requires an additional subscription that provides access to the British censuses, Vital Records (Civil Registration) along with WW1 and WW2 military records.

The other social networking websites all allow an interexchange in a similar way but have no additional historical records to search. Each website has millions of members and many individuals belong to multiple communities which increase their chances of locating additional data and new family members.

Chapter 14

Family History Games

To date most of the Family History/Genealogy games created have been done on an individual family level in hopes of interesting the next generation. The emphasis has always been on sharing ancestral stories at family gatherings.

Some individuals have created playing cards with pictures of ancestors on one side and a little history on the other side. Sitting with a child and going through them or allowing the child to browse through them will help them to learn about their ancestors. Others have created 'Old Maid' type games like *Amy* did on her blog *Teach Mama.*[31]

———————————————

[31] "family photos + playing cards = three games!." teach mama — learning in the every day.
http://teachmama.com/2009/12/family-photos-playing-cards-three-games.html (accessed January 20, 2011).

I printed everyone's picture twice, using the 'wallet' size option, and they fit perfectly on the cards. I used cardstock for both the pictures and playing cards.

I cut out the cards and pictures, then glued the pictures onto the cards. I then wrapped the cards in clear contact paper, and I was finished.

If we hadn't just had a million snow days and my husband could have made it into school, he would have laminated everything for me. Plan B was to use clear contact paper, and it worked out fine.

http://teachmama.com/2009/12/family-photos-playing-cards-three-games.html

Facebook.com has some applications to help build family trees. The chart below shows all of the applications available as of January, 2011. As with all things technological, someone new will create another interesting game or feature to enhance what is currently available; this is one of the great benefits of open source today. To learn more about *Open Source* go to http://www.opensource.org/ and learn how individuals share and exchange program codes.

Each of them contributes to extending family trees in different ways. As these are new ideas on ways to locate new family members, time will tell if they are successful.

While writing this book, a new game was announced in the newspapers and has appeared on Facebook entitled *Family Village*. It is still in the early stages but it promises to be a way to interest varying age levels in building their family tree.

As an individual begins the game, they are given a character that represents them. Slowly the individual adds other family members and completes various tasks and jobs that earns money and builds homes. As new members are added, documents from *FamilyLink* are added as sources backing up the existence of the added person.

The center has a 'Heritage Tree' which grows as you add more family members. Visiting the library in the village allows access to more documents *FamilyLink* locates for the individuals. The opportunity to work with others or connect with others who are also participating has not become evident yet as this program has just barely been released. It will be interesting to take another look at this program in a

year after it matures and becomes fully functional.

As this is a new area in Family History there

may be other online games that are worth discussing

or mentioning please feel free to contact the authors

and let us know.

Conclusion

Genealogists have been tracing family history lines for generations; always with the tools available at the time. Different time periods introduced new ways to quicken the pace of this endeavor to the point where within in few mouse clicks an individual can view a copy of an original document from the 1500s to more modern times.

Originally these documents were only available to the qualified few and were handled with care in order to preserve them. Digitizing these valuable records has accomplished preservation and accessibility by anyone.

Where distance was a barrier, today's technological improvements have created a borderless internet where individuals may come together, become friends, discover relationships, exchange family data and all from the comfort of their home at any time of the day.

The phrase of "Who Am I" quickly disintegrates with the discovery of each new ancestor. Expanding one's family with new found cousins adds to their makeup. When pictures and stories are exchanged, miles and miles apart as well as time periods, uncanny similarities are also found and often family ties are strengthened in the process.

Family History research has no age limitations, from the young to the old, everyone has a story to tell, everyone wants to connect to the human family of those past and present. The everyday lives shared through social networking are interwoven and often similar regardless of location, age or any other man made barrier that occurs in the physical presence.

As individuals read through the pages of this book, may they learn and use the new tools available to extend their ancestral research as well as strengthening their own family ties.

Index

www.ingramcontent.com/pod-product-compliance
Lightning Source LLC
Chambersburg PA
CBHW051249050326
40689CB00007B/1121